His Grace is Enough

*True Freedom and Belonging comes
from your identity in Christ*

Christine Marie Emelone

Christine Marie Emelone

Kingdom Publishers

www.kingdompublishers.co.uk

His Grace is Enough

Copyright © Christine Marie Emelone

All rights reserved.

No part of this book may be reproduced in any form by photocopying or any electronic or mechanical means, including information storage or retrieval systems, without permission in writing from both the copyright owner and the publisher of the book. The right of Christine Marie Emelone to be identified as the author of this work has been asserted by him/her in accordance with the Copyright, Designs and Patents Act 1988 and any subsequent amendments thereto. A catalogue record for this book is available from the British Library.

ISBN: 978-1-913247-31-7

1st Edition by Kingdom Publishers
Kingdom Publishers
London, UK.

You can purchase copies of this book from any leading bookstore or email contact@kingdompublishers.co.uk

Dedication

I would like to dedicate this book to my older brother, and pray that he comes to know of God's love and that his true identity, belonging and fulfilment is found in Christ

Contents

Chapter 1 - *Our Identity in Christ* — 7

Chapter 2 - *A Promise and a Choice* — 11

Chapter 3 - *Feeling Afraid* — 17

Chapter 4 - *Schemes of the Enemy* — 22

Chapter 5 - *Chosen to Serve* — 28

Chapter 6 - *He is with Us* — 34

Chapter 7 - *Motivated by Love* — 39

Chapter 8 - *He Paid the Price* — 43

Introduction

Humanity is obsessed with purpose. The search to find belonging, fulfilment and freedom in your identity is never-ending. The truth is all these things cannot be found outside your identity in Christ. It is pointless to look elsewhere to find your purpose and who you are because it is not actually possible. The only way to find true freedom, fulfilment and your identity dwells within Jesus. Because of Him, you can become the person He created you to be, as well as feel free to be yourself.

'His grace is enough' explores how lasting joy and peace are found in who we are in Christ and what this means for us. It reminds us that we have been specially chosen by God to serve and glorify Him in everything we do. Embedded in our hearts should be a deep and genuine desire to build and encourage others. This book explains how God's promises and love for us should affect how we live our lives, the choices we make and the way we love others.

I wrote this book because I wanted to send a message out to those who are struggling with identity, belonging and purpose. Hopefully, this book will remind them of how they are loved, valued and cherished by God. He has a plan and purpose for our lives that is beyond what we can imagine and is not to be taken lightly. I expect this book to be used as a guide to see why God has called us, who He says we are, and what He wants for us in our lives. It can also be used as a book to 'dip in and out' of, as there are many Bible verses to describe and help to explain what God is saying to us and why it is important for us as believers.

From this book, I pray that you come to know of God's love which will fuel your love for others. I hope you will believe that God is always with us and will never leave or abandon us, even when times are hard.

Psalm 139:14
'I will praise You, for I am fearfully and wonderfully made; Your works are wonderful, I know that full well.'

Chapter 1
Our Identity in Christ

It is common and easy for us to spend our time worrying about what people think of us. We desire to be loved, respected and seen as people who are fun, vibrant and lively. We begin to lose sight of how much we need Jesus, in contrast to positive comments and approval of other flawed beings. The fact is, God's view of who we are is the only one which matters, and we should refuse to place our sense of self-worth and identity on what other people think of us.

Galatians 1:10
'Am I now trying to win the approval of human beings, or of God? Or am I trying to please people? If I were still trying to please people, I would not be a servant of Christ.'

One misconception that many people believe about the Christian life is that it is boring and cannot provide true fulfilment. They tend to go on a search for things they believe will make them feel happy or fulfilled. The truth is, none of the things the world has to offer can truly satisfy, and lasting joy, peace and contentment dwell within the Christian life.

All the worldly things which may look appealing and promise fulfilment are actually counterfeit, as they can leave you feeling empty and discontented. To summarise, we cannot find true fulfilment or freedom outside our identity in Christ.

So, the question is, who are we in Christ?

1 Peter 2:9

'But you are a chosen people, a royal priesthood, a holy nation, God's special possession that you may declare the praises of Him who called you out of the darkness into His wonderful light.'

Say this to yourself:

'I am chosen. God chose me because He loves me. He called me out of the darkness into His wonderful light.'

We are God's special possession, carefully chosen by Him to declare His glory. Highly valued and loved, He called us out into the light and wants us to serve Him with everything we have. With confidence and certainty, we can come to God and ask for wisdom, faith and guidance about any situation or fear in our hearts.

We gain a new identity and a brand-new life through His salvation which should lead us to put Jesus first in our lives, behave in a godly way and have a new outlook on things as a result of how He has changed us.

2 Corinthians 5:7

'This means that anyone who belongs to Christ has become a new person. The old life is gone; a new life has begun!'

As believers, we must note that this does not simply mean an improved or better version of ourselves. We have been set apart, washed and completely cleansed from all our impurities. Our new identity completely changes our relationship with God as He has made us a new creation, and we are to be transformed and made anew by God's love.

Matthew 5:14

'You are the light of the world. A town built on a hill cannot be hidden. Neither do people light a lamp and put it under a bowl. Instead, they put it on its stand, and it gives light to everyone in the house. In the same way, let your light shine before others.'

God created us to be different. He wants us to stand out from the crowd and let our light shine. We were not designed to follow the world and its ways, but to reflect Jesus at work in our lives. Although it may be difficult at times, we should be confident to stand for Jesus and set an example for others by living the way Jesus did.

Romans 8:37

'No, in all these things we are more than conquerors through Him who loved us.'

Thinking Time

How do these Bible verses from Ephesians show how we should respond to Jesus and live our lives because of our identity in Him?

Ephesians 5:8-10

'For you were once darkness, but now you are light in the Lord. Live as children of light (for the fruit of the light consists in all goodness, righteousness and truth) and find out what pleases the Lord.'

Ephesians 4:1-2

'As a prisoner for the Lord, then, I urge you to live a life worthy of the calling you have received. Be completely humble and gentle, bearing with one another in love.'

Ephesians 4:22-24

'You were taught, with regard to your former way of life, to put off your old self, which is being corrupted by its deceitful desires; to be made new in the attitude of your minds; and to put on the new self, created to be like God in true righteousness and holiness.'

Lord,

Thank You calling me out of the darkness into your wonderful light. I am so grateful that I am specially chosen by You to declare Your glory and sing of Your praises. Thank You for making me different and unique to those around me. Please help me to focus on who You say I am, rather than what other people think about me. Help me to respond to Your love by living a life pleasing to You and finding true fulfilment from my identity in Christ. Lead me to find true peace, joy and satisfaction in Jesus.

Chapter 2
A Promise and a Choice

Imagine God is an artist who gives us a blank canvas with the ability to create whatever we wish, the way that we desire. As painters, the choice in our hands, we can draw our own lives and fumble with the paintbrush of life or let God design our lives.

As believers, it is imperative for us to remain thoughtful about the way we decide to paint our lives.

Ephesians 2:10
'For we are God's masterpiece. He created us anew in Christ Jesus, so we can do the things He planned for us long ago.'

God says we are the result of His artistic skills. We were not just randomly placed, but we are valuable, special and carefully made.

Our lifestyle choices and the decisions we make will prove the sincerity of our claims to love Jesus. Realistically, there are only two choices: to live with, or without, Jesus in your life.

Matthew 7:13

'Enter through the narrow gate. For wide is the gate and broad is the road that leads to destruction, and many enter through it. But small is the gate and narrow the road that leads to life, and only a few find it.'

The path to heaven is not an easy path. Jesus describes it as narrow, and only a few find it. This path involves putting God first, trusting in His Word and standing in the faith.

Needless to say, this contrasts with the wide gate which is the easy and carefree lifestyle which involves putting yourself at the centre, not worrying about the consequences of your actions, and doing as you wish. It looks appealing and attractive to the eyes and you have enough room to do what you want, how you want. There is no Jesus in the picture, but it is full of self-love and pride.

There are two questions I want you to ask yourself:

Am I willing and ready to follow Jesus?

What price am I willing to pay?

We see in the Book of John where Jesus talks with a Samaritan woman at the well. This woman was looked down upon by her people and ostracised by society. She was an outcast, given no respect and marked as immoral. Traditionally, the Jews despised Samaritans and viewed them as a race which had no claim on their God.

During Biblical times, women were known to chat and socialise when drawing water from the well and it was a highlight of their day. As the Samaritan woman comes to draw water from the well alone, she was shunned by the community and not welcome in society.

Starting with a simple request, we see how Jesus subtly leads this Samaritan woman forward until she not only yearns for salvation but gains a hunger and thirst for a relationship with God.

John 4:7
'When a Samaritan woman came to draw water, Jesus said to her, "Will you give me a drink?"'

Notably, Jesus uses the words 'Will you' and not 'You have to', showing how coming to Jesus is a choice that we should want to make and not feel forced or pressurised to. When Jesus asks the Samaritan woman for a drink at the well, she does not see it as a simple request of human kindness. In her response, she becomes defensive and even suspicious of Jesus:

John 4:9
"'You are a Jew and I am a Samaritan woman. How can you ask me for a drink?'"

Evidently, the walls of resentment, mistrust and uncertainty put up by the Samaritan woman were thick and high. At the initial stage, she was reluctant to open her heart to God. Undoubtedly, the fact that she highlights Jesus being a Jew and their refusal to associate with Samaritans showed how Jesus was reaching across a vast distance to this Samaritan woman. But Jesus makes a claim about Himself and the water He provides which draws the woman in and changes her heart.

John 4:13
'Everyone who drinks this water will be thirsty again, but whoever drinks the water I give them will never thirst. Indeed, the water I give them will become in them a spring of water welling up to eternal life.'

Jesus is freely offering the promise and gift of eternal life to whoever comes to Him. It is important to understand that it is only through Jesus that this wonderful gift is given. He is not one of many ways, but the only way to receive it.

Also, we should note how Jesus says we will 'never thirst again.' This is not a temporary, short-term reward which only lasts a while and then is gone, but a gift which lasts forever that can never be taken from us.

John 4:15

'The woman said to him, "Sir, give me this water so that I won't get thirsty and have to keep coming here to draw water."'

The Samaritan woman yearned for this type of water because she wanted to have eternal life - a gift that would truly satisfy her soul's desire. Her encounter with Jesus at the well meant her life completely changed and could not remain the same. She was willing to change and accept God into her life and receive a gift beyond her understanding and imagination.

Thinking Time

What do these Bible verses tell us about God's promises and rewards to us if we follow Him?

Hebrews 11:6

'And without faith it is impossible to please God, because anyone who comes to Him must believe that He exists and that He rewards those who earnestly seek Him.'

Colossians 3:3-4

'For you died, and your life is now hidden with Christ in God. When Christ, who is your life, appears, then you also will appear with Him in glory.'

Matthew 16:27

'For the Son of Man is going to come in His Father's glory with his angels, and then He will reward each person according to what they have done.'

Lord,

Thank You that because of You, I will never thirst again, and I can receive living waters. I am so grateful for the gift of eternal life which You offer to anyone who genuinely comes to You. Thank You that I am no longer enslaved to sin but freed by Your precious blood on the cross. I pray you would keep me close to You and open my eyes to times when I forget and dismiss my need for You. Please help me to walk on the right path and make godly decisions which are pleasing to You. Help me to paint a picture in my life reflecting Jesus, and Him at work in me. Show me how to serve, glorify and work for You only.

Chapter 3
Feeling Afraid

When we face trials and temptations, we inevitably feel alone, and it becomes hard to rest in God's promises. Feelings of doubt, fear and anxiety begin to take a hold over us, and we lose sight of how much God loves us and cares about us. The key to overcoming fear and feeling afraid is our complete trust in God. This means that we turn to God even in the most difficult times, believing He has everything under control. He reminds us in His Word that we can depend on Him with our lives and cast everything in our hearts onto Him because He loves us.

Matthew 6:26-34
'Look at the birds of the air, for they do not sow or reap or store away in barns, and yet your heavenly Father feeds them. Are you not much more valuable than they? Can any of you by worrying add a single hour to your life?'

God tells us not to spend our time worrying about the future. We are to focus on praying and trusting in Him as well as remaining in His Word.

An example of a prominent figure in the Old Testament who was afraid, and yet God called him to make his mark as a strong, confident figure, is Moses. Otherwise known as the Giver of the Law, Moses led the Israelites into the Promised

Land and out of captivity in Egypt, informed Pharaoh of the Ten Plagues of God's judgement upon the land of Egypt and went up Mount Sinai to collect the Ten Commandments.

The life of Moses is definitely worth looking at when feeling afraid in our walk with God. Exodus chapters 3 and 4 give us an enormous insight into the way in which Moses reacted to the crucial challenge presented to him by God.

A key experience which changes Moses' life completely is his encounter with God at the burning bush. Undeniably, Moses was full of fear but followed God's commands whilst trusting in Him. We see when God calls out to Moses and he responds with 'Here I am.' (v4)

I want you to ask yourself these questions:

How do I respond to Jesus when I am feeling afraid?

Do I trust in Him when I feel scared or alone?

In Exodus 3-4, we see how God appears to Moses and calls him to be a saviour of the people of Egypt.

Exodus 3:6
'Then he said, "I am the God of your father, the God of Abraham, the God of Isaac and the God of Jacob." At this Moses hid his face, because he was afraid to look at God.'

Just as we probably would have felt, Moses was scared to face God and as a natural response, hid his face from Him. It goes without saying that being in the presence of God changes everything and as a result, Moses would never remain the same after his experience.

Exodus 3:11
'But Moses said to God, "Who am I that I should go to Pharaoh and bring the Israelites out of Egypt?"'

The response that Moses gives to God shows that he is afraid of the responsibility being given to him. He doesn't feel like God has chosen the right person or that he is the one meant for the role. In other words, Moses is asking, 'Why me? How can I face the Pharaoh? Who am I to be a leader and represent the people of Egypt?'

Sometimes, we can feel like Moses in the sense that we feel afraid to go out of our comfort zone, make sacrifices, and go the extra mile when serving God. It is common and normal for this to happen, and God does not think any less of us or believe that we are less skilled but comforts us and brings us in to His never-ending love.

Exodus 4:10
'Moses said to the Lord, "Pardon your servant, Lord. I have never been eloquent, neither in the past nor since you have spoken to your servant. I am slow of speech and tongue."'

Moses begins to give reasons why he cannot obey God because he is afraid and scared that he will not be able to fulfil his calling. He starts to focus on his weaknesses and things he thinks will hinder him from following God, rather than trusting in God and concentrating on what He is asking him to do.

Exodus 4:13
'But Moses said, "Pardon your servant Lord. Please send someone else."'

Even though God has assured Moses that He will be with him (Exodus 3:12), Moses still does not feel fit to be a leader and ready for the task God has called him to do. Sometimes we can fall into the same way of thinking; it is difficult when God's thoughts and ways are not like ours, and we fail to think beyond our own reasoning and what we believe to be true.

Say this to yourself:

I do not have to feel afraid. Jesus is with me and promises to never let me go. I can rest assured that there is peace, contentment and endless joy in His everlasting love.

Thinking Time

How do these Bible verses show us that we can trust in Jesus when we feel afraid?

Isaiah 41:10

'Fear not, for I am with you; be not dismayed, for I am your God; I will strengthen you, I will help you, I will uphold you with my righteous right hand.'

Psalm 91

'Whoever dwells in the shelter of the Most High will rest in the shadow of the Almighty. I will say to the Lord, "He is my refuge and my fortress, my God in whom I trust."'

Psalm 91:4

'He will cover you with His feathers and under His wings you will find refuge.'

Hebrews 13:6

'So we can confidently say, "The Lord is my helper; I will not fear; what can man do to me?"'

Lord,

Thank You that I no longer have to feel afraid and fearful but can find true joy and peace in You. Help me to completely trust and draw closer to You during times when I feel scared and alone. Please give me faith, courage and confidence to stand for Jesus. Help me to be bold and firm in what I believe. Let Your Word be a light to my path and guide me through trials and temptations that I face.

Chapter 4
Schemes of the Enemy

There are many ways in which Satan is described in the Scriptures: prince of the air, father of lies, tempter, deceiver, the list goes on. A common way the enemy corrupts and wreaks havoc in our lives is through deception.

Some of the potent lies Satan tells are as follows: God's grace is not enough; we cannot overcome our fleshly desires; and joy is found in having more things. When he accomplishes deceiving us, he gains power and authority in our lives.

The most effective way for us as believers to resist the devil is to read and study the Scriptures, remind ourselves who God is and His promises for us. We should also remember to come to God in prayer and ask for faith and wisdom.

By knowing Satan's schemes in attacking our faith, we become more equipped to resist and take a stand against him. Since he can deceive Adam and Eve to sin and fall from God's goodness, there is no doubt that he is a worthy opponent for which we need to be prepared.

1) Satan wants us to believe God's grace is not enough Contrary to Scripture, the enemy wants you to think that Jesus's death on the cross was not enough to cover all your sins, past, present and future, but only covers some of them.

It is imperative for us to go to the Word for truth, so we do not fall into the trap of believing the enemy's lies. In Peter 4:8, we are reminded that 'Above all, love each other deeply, because love covers a multitude of sins.'

Jesus showed us the depth of His love for us by bearing all, not some, of our iniquities on the cross. This undeniable act of love demonstrates how Jesus covered our sins by forgiveness and love, by sacrificing Himself for us on the cross.

2) The enemy knows the Bible but uses it for his own agenda
Without a doubt, it will be surprising for many people to know that Satan is well aware and versed in God's Word. In the Book of Matthew, we see how Jesus is tempted by the devil after fasting for forty days and forty nights.

Satan's second attempt to tempt Jesus is to convince Him to throw Himself down from the highest point of the temple in the holy city. Since he failed to tempt Jesus the first time, he turns to quoting from the Bible, as he is fully aware of its authority appealed to by God. Using scripture, Satan tries to manipulate Jesus for his own agenda and aims.

Matthew 4:6
"'If you are the Son of God," he said, "throw yourself down. For it is written: 'He will command his angels

concerning you, and they will lift you up in their hands, so that you will not strike your foot against a stone'."

By changing and misinterpreting the psalm, Satan uses the Bible to try and achieve his evil purposes. In his schemes to trip us up in our walk with Christ, he twists God's Word subtly in an attack to weaken and debilitate our faith. The devil's agenda here was to get Jesus to make the mistake to fall because of pride, just as he had done. The devil knows there is no redemption for him as he was cast down by God and wanted Jesus to be just like him by casting Himself down.

We must note that as Christians, simply knowing scriptures is not enough because the enemy is also fully aware of what the Word says, but this calls for interpreting what the Bible says in its full context for effective use against the enemy.

3) Satan wants us to believe we cannot overcome our fleshly desires
Even though the Bible clearly states that we can resist our fleshly desires, the enemy wants us to indulge in sin and believe that there is nothing wrong with putting our own desires first. Satan wants us to become the god of ourselves and be more self-seeking, which is idolatry and opposed by God (Exodus 20:3-5).

Galatians 5:16-17
'So I say, live by the Spirit, and you will not gratify the desires of the flesh. For the flesh desires what is contrary to the Spirit, and the Spirit what is contrary to the flesh.'

Satan aims to plant seeds of doubt into our mind and remind of us our past, so we are not able to focus on our future and the plans God has for our lives. He wants us to drift further and further away from Jesus and for our mindset to turn to thoughts of 'I can't', such as 'I can't pray, I can't come to Jesus'.

The devil dresses up sin, ties it with a ribbon and tries to make it look pretty and attractive without letting you see sin as it is - damaging, harmful and self-seeking. It is a counterfeit trap which promises fulfilment and joy but essentially leads to ruin.

Because of the shame one can feel from sin, Satan wants us to feel like it is not possible for us to be fully loved by God and as a result of this, we walk away from our faith and do not want to make ourselves fully known to Him by not praying or having a relationship with Him.

4) The devil wants us to think joy is found in having more things
After failing to successfully tempt Jesus twice, the devil takes

Him to a very high mountain to show Him the kingdoms of the world in their splendour and says this:

Matthew 4:9
"'All this I will give you," he said, "if you will bow down and worship me.'"

The enemy wants us to think that true joy comes from the material things that we have, so we essentially begin to place our trust in our possessions. Satan wants us to believe that having faith in possessions will make us content. He does not want us to know that the things of this world are temporary, short-term things which will eventually fade.

Jesus clearly states in the Word that, 'Life does not consist in an abundance of possessions.' (Luke 12:15)

Thinking Time

How can we apply these Bible verses about resisting the enemy coming into our lives?

Ephesians 6:11
'Put on the full armour of God so that you will be able to stand firm against the schemes of the devil.'

James 4:7
'Submit yourselves to God. Resist the devil and he will flee from you.'

1 Peter 5:8-9

'Be alert and of sober mind. Your enemy, the devil, prowls around like a roaring lion looking for someone to devour. Resist him, standing firm in the faith, because you know that the family of believers in the world is undergoing the same kind of sufferings.'

Lord,

Thank You for giving us the Word so we can stand firm and bold against the devil's schemes. Thank You for setting an example and showing us how to live our lives. Help me to grow in my faith and walk with Christ. Please give me wisdom, faith and understanding so I do not give in to Satan's lies and fall for his schemes. Guide me to paths which serve and glorify You. Please forgive me during times when I sin and do things which do not please You. Help me to come back to You in faith and trust whenever I have fears and feel afraid and alone.

Chapter 5
Chosen to Serve

Many tend to think that you can pick and choose when to serve Christ and it is easier to serve Christ when things are going well compared to when times are tough and hard. The Bible instructs us to praise and worship God during all seasons, and we are not to cherry-pick when we serve God.

Romans 14:8
'If we live, we live for the Lord; and if we die, we die for the Lord. So, whether we live or die, we belong to the Lord.'

We belong to Christ regardless of our situation and we have been chosen to serve, glorify and praise Him only.

To be a servant of Christ means to work selflessly and humbly, with only one motive - to please God. This involves a life full of prayer and holiness, meditating in His Word, gratifying the desires of the Spirit, and obedience to Him only. It can be hard to serve Jesus during difficult times, but a servant of Christ will trust in Him for wisdom in trials and temptations, believing that He will never leave them even when they feel alone.

Christian living is at the heart of Christian servanthood. Our words and songs are meaningless if they are not matched with our lives and how we serve and love others. When we make small decisions everyday which glorify God, we are essentially training our hearts to work for Jesus.

For example, when we look at the life of Daniel, he was living in a time where the Babylonian society chose to live as they pleased and had a strong self-seeking attitude to life.

Without a doubt, this would have made life for Daniel very difficult as he sought to please God and put Him first. Being surrounded by people who didn't care about God would have been challenging. The temptation he would have faced would have been to compromise what he believed about God.

But Daniel did not complain that the pressure was too much or debate whether it was acceptable for him to compromise on his beliefs. Not at all, because Daniel knew whom he served. He refused to serve the king's orders to eat the royal food and wine and follow the Babylonian ways and ate vegetables instead.

Daniel 1:12-13
"'Please test your servants for ten days: Give us nothing but vegetables to eat and water to drink. Then compare our appearance with that of the young men who eat the royal food.'"

Standing firm and strong, he refused to defile himself with the royal food and wine. After ten days, Daniel and his companions came out healthier and more well-nourished than the young men eating royal food. It was not meant to turn out like that, but God was with them throughout the trial and never left them.

Say this to yourself:

God called me to serve Him. I can serve Jesus with confidence in the face of consequences. When times are hard, I can trust Him for faith and wisdom to lead me to do what is right.

The desire from a true servant's heart to please Jesus will lead them to look forward to when they enter their Heavenly Father's arms and receive His approval.

Matthew 25:21
'Well done, good and faithful servant. Enter into the joy of your Master!'

To say you are a servant of Christ but are pretentious and self-seeking would be a disservice to God, who cannot be mocked, and knows the false from the true servants and the bad fruit from the good.

Luke 6:46
"'Why do you call me, 'Lord, Lord' and not do what I say?'"

Matthew 20:28
'Just as the Son of Man did not come to be served, but to serve and to give His life as a ransom for many.'

An example of how Jesus served is when he washed the feet of his disciples in the Book of John. Although they followed and served Him only, we see Him committing a humble act as He displays His humility. This also foreshadowed His ultimate act of love for us on the cross.

In the first century of Israel, it was essential that feet were washed before a meal due to the filthy roads and many wearing sandals.

In John 13:4, we see Jesus carrying out the work of the lowliest of servants as He rose from the table, tied a towel around His waist and began to wash His disciples' feet. Undoubtedly, Jesus stooping to this level would have shocked the disciples into silence, but it also confused them about why their leader was stooping so low.

From this, how do we know we are chosen to serve?

John 13:15
'For I have given you an example, that you also should do just as I have done to you.'

Jesus was setting the ground-rules of how we are to serve others in the same way that He did. As followers of Christ, we should have a genuine want to build others up and encourage them out of love.

Thinking Time

How do these Bible verses show why serving God is important?

What are the different ways we can serve others?

John 12:26
'Whoever serves me must follow me; and where I am, my servant also will be. My father will honour the one who serves me.'

1 Peter 4:10
'Each of you should use whatever gift you have received to serve others, as faithful stewards of God's grace in its various forms.'

Hebrews 10:24-25

'And let us consider how we may spur one another on towards love and good deeds, not giving up meeting together as some are in the habit of doing but encouraging one another - and all the more as we see the Day approaching.'

Lord,

Thank You for coming to this world and setting an example for how I am to serve others. Forgive me when I am self-seeking or act in an ungodly way. I pray You would grant me a serving heart which is full of grace and love for You. Please keep my wandering heart focused on You so that I do not drift from Your Word. Show me how to serve others in a way which is glorifying to You. Help me to be humble and put others before myself.

Chapter 6
He is with Us

We are not left on our own to tackle the problems and troubles life throws at us. Sometimes we may feel alone during hard times and think that God is silent or not watching over us. The instant we accept Jesus into our lives, He gives us the Holy Spirit to guide and lead us through life.

John 14:15-15
'If you love me, keep my commands. And I will ask the Father, and He will give you another advocate to help you and be with you for ever - The Spirit of Truth.'

Hebrews 4:15
'For we do not have a high priest who is unable to feel sympathy for our weaknesses, but we have one who has been tempted in every way, just as we are - yet He did not sin.'

Jesus has experienced and been through every temptation we may face. Whatever sin we may be struggling with - lust, pride, anger etc, He understands our individual battles and will never leave us on our own. He is walking with us in our trials, holding our hands tightly just like a Heavenly Father would. He promises to never abandon us no matter how we may feel.

Imagine life being like a staircase. God is able to see, control and change the entire staircase but we can only see one step at a time. We are free in the sense that we can make choices in our moves, but we are limited as to how much of the staircase we can see. As we make our move, God is guiding us through our lives and unfolding the next step, one step at a time.

Say this to yourself:

I do not have to face the troubles of life alone because Jesus is walking with me. I can have faith in Him to carry me through hard times. I can be sure of His perfect love for me.

In the Book of Luke, we see when large crowds were travelling with Jesus and He turned to them and said this:

'If anyone comes to me and does not hate father and mother, wife and children, brothers and sisters - yes, even their own life - such a person cannot be my disciple. And whoever does not carry their cross and follow me cannot be my disciple.'

Undoubtedly, there is a great sacrifice that comes when trying to do a great thing.

An example of God showing He will never abandon His children regardless of the situation can be found in the story of Shadrach, Meshach and Abednego. They refused to follow the orders of the king and worship his image because God was first in their hearts.

Daniel 3:12

'But there are some Jews whom you have set over the affairs of the province of Babylon - Shadrach, Meshach and Abednego - who pay no attention you, Your Majesty. They neither serve your gods nor worship the image of gold you have set up.'

It is not surprising that this enraged the king who would severely punish them as he wanted to be worshipped. Before Shadrach, Meshach and Abednego were thrown into the blazing furnace, they still had faith in Jesus regardless of whether they survived or not.

Daniel 3:17-18

'If we are thrown into the blazing furnace, the God we serve is able to deliver us from it, and He will deliver us from Your Majesty's hand. But even if He does not, we want you to know, Your Majesty, that we will not worship your gods or worship the image of gold you have set up.'

We should note how they said, 'even if He does not'. Our faith in Jesus means that we can have confidence in the face of consequences. This does not mean that they were not feeling afraid or scared about their situation, but they gave their lives to Jesus trusting He was able to rescue them and bring them out of the furnace. Just as they believed, God never left them, and He was walking with them in the fire.

Daniel 3:25
'Look! I see four men walking around in the fire, unbound and unharmed, and the fourth looks like a son of the gods.'

Thinking Time

How can we be sure that Jesus is with us from these Bible verses?

Deuteronomy 31:8
'It is the Lord who goes before you. He will be with you; He will not leave you or forsake you. Do not fear or be dismayed.'

Matthew 28:20
'Teaching them to obey everything I have commanded you. And surely, I am with you always, to the very end of this age.'

Zephaniah 3:17

'The Lord your God is in your midst, a mighty one who will save; He will rejoice over you with gladness; He will quiet you by his love; He will exult you over with loud singing.'

Lord,

Thank You for giving me the Holy Spirit to guide and lead me through life and make decisions which glorify You. Thank You for the lives of Shadrach, Meshach and Abednego teaching me that I can have confidence in the face of consequences. Please help me not to feel scared and afraid, but to have courage knowing You are walking with me through any trials I may face. Help me to trust and believe that I can come to You with any fear or situation knowing that You understand and will never leave my side.

Chapter 7
Motivated by Love

God's love for us is at the heart of the gospel. Our love for God will show a love for people. Embedded in our hearts should be a godly desire to build and encourage others. As believers, the Bible tells us not to focus on ourselves but to show love in the same way that we received it from Jesus. We should be fuelled by his unique love for us.

To be a follower of Christ comes at a cost. Jesus is saying that we must be fully ready to place Him at the centre of our hearts and essentially, hand over everything to do with us, about us, and in us, to Him. To take this step back requires a lot of prayer, humility and faith which we can always look to God for and find in His Word.

A common response to this that appears often is we would love to do what God has called us to but as soon as we hear that it comes at cost we move further and further away from Him because we are not willing to pay the price. It is easy for us to remain in places where we feel comfortable and loved, but moving away from these environments can seem daunting. Jesus calls us to go the extra mile when we love others and be prepared to put others before ourselves.

Most of the time, it can be easier to love ourselves than to love others and, as fallen creatures, this can stem from selfishness or an unwilling attitude to put others first. Due to sin, we can find it difficult to love others, but the Bible tells us to be humble and always show love to others.

Philippians 2:3
'Do nothing out of selfish ambition or vain conceit. Rather, in humility value others before yourselves, not looking to your own interests but each of you to the interests of others.'

When we misinterpret the true meaning of love, we can find it extremely hard to love others. Love is often thought of as a solely emotional response which is based on feelings. But feelings can change, and we serve a Heavenly Father who never changes and forever remains the same.

The type of love God has for us is referred to as agape love in Greek, which basically means sacrificial love. In the midst of our sin, God died for us on the cross so we that we could be with Him and have eternal life. Even at our worst, His unending love caused Him to sacrifice Himself for us. This is the type of love God wants us to have for others. Not love based on emotion and feeling, but agape love which genuinely comes from the heart because our response to what our Saviour did for us on the cross fuels our love for others. We become humble, loving.

Ephesians 5:1
'Follow God's example, therefore, as dearly loved children and live a life of love, just as Christ loved us and gave Himself up for us as a fragrant offering and sacrifice to God.'

God doesn't command us to 'Feel love towards others', He wants it to be a part of how we live our lives. He wants us to follow His steps and example of agape love. This doesn't mean we are to literally go on a cross, but we are to love others enough to sacrifice for them, regardless of how we may be feeling.

1 John 3:16
'This is how we know what love is: Jesus Christ laid down His life for us.'

Thinking Time

What do these Bible verses say about loving others?

1 John 4: 11
'Dear friends, since God so loved us, we ought to love one another. No one has ever seen God; but if we love one another, God lives in us and His love is made complete in us.'

Also, we are to love our enemies the same way we love our friends. This can be difficult at times when we are in situations that can cause us to sin, but the Bible says we are to trust in Jesus. Most importantly, we are to reflect Him in everything we do.

Luke 6:27

'Love your enemies, do good to those who hate you, bless those who curse you, pray for those who ill-treat you.'

Luke 6:32

'If you love those who love you, what credit is that to you? Even sinners love those who love them.'

Lord,

Thank You for Your sacrificial love on the cross. Thank You for Your mercy and grace which You give freely to all who earnestly seek You. Help me to love others the way Jesus loved and not be something I do reluctantly or because I feel like I have to, but because of Jesus' unconditional love for me. Please lead me in Your love to those around me and fill me with a pure, serving heart which longs for You. I am sorry for the times when I turn away from Your love and distance myself from having a relationship with You. Please God, forgive me for the times when I am unloving or self-seeking and show me how to make decisions and choice which please You.

Chapter 8
He Paid the Price

It is common for us to feel as though after we have made a mistake or done something wrong, there is no coming back from our misdeeds and that nothing can change what we have done. Similarly, to our prayer lives, when we sin, it becomes easy to think things like:

'I messed up so I can't pray today.'

'I'm not worthy enough to pray.'

'God is angry with me.'

However, this is not how it works with our Heavenly Father. The truth is that we are bound to sin, it is impossible to go a day without sinning. But this does not mean all hope is lost. We serve a forgiving and loving Father whose mercies are new every morning, (Lamentations 3:22-23) and He freely gives His love to all who genuinely come to Him as they are.

The misconception often comes that doing good works and living a godly life is the only way He will love and accept you, but we must understand that it is not about what we do for God or how much we do it, but about what He has already come and done for us. This is not to say that we should not be obedient and live godly lives, as this what we are called to do, but out of genuine love for what our Saviour did for us. It is our response to His selfless, perfect love that causes us to remain in grateful obedience for His glory and pleasure.

Imagine God being like the Sun. Jesus steps in and clothes us with a pure, clean garment so we can withstand being in God's presence. He has paid the price of our sins by giving Himself up on the cross. Because we choose to place our faith in Him, we are guaranteed salvation and eternal life with Christ. God sees us the same way He sees Jesus - blameless and pure.

On the contrary, if we do not believe in Jesus and were to stand before God, we would just burn up because of our refusal to accept Jesus Christ as saviour.

Romans 6:23
'For the wages of sin is death.'

Ultimately, the punishment for sin is death and everyone has deserved eternal separation from God in hell because of our sin. God does not overlook or take sin lightly.

In the Garden of Eden, when Adam and Eve sinned by disobeying God's instructions, God had to punish them. From Adam's sin, everyone has been guilty of sinning against God and rebelling against His righteous laws.

Although we are bound to die both physically and spiritually, God has mercifully given us a way out of this problem - the blood of His blameless and perfect Son on the cross. Through Jesus, the gift of eternity with God becomes available to all believers - those who genuinely trust and put their faith in Christ. We should note that the two components which are undeniably key to being saved are having faith and believing that Jesus died on the cross for all our sins.

The price Jesus paid on our behalf reveals to us the depth of how terrible and broken the nature of our sin was. The only way the remission of our sins is possible is through Jesus' blood on the cross and trusting in our pure and sinless saviour whose death was reserved to pay our debt once and for all.

Psalm 103:12
'As far as the east is from the west, so far He has removed our transgressions from us.'

Romans 8:38
'For I am convinced that neither death nor life, neither angels nor demons, neither the present nor the future, nor any powers, neither height nor depth, nor anything else in creation, will be able to separate us from the love of God that is in Christ Jesus our Lord.'

This long list, which Paul states, shows us that God loves us conditionally regardless of what we are facing in life or things which may make us feel intimidated or afraid. We can rest assured that God is walking with his children, teaching and guiding them, just as a Heavenly Father would.

Thinking Time

What can we learn from these Bible verses about Jesus paying the price for us?

Hebrews 10:10
'And by that will, we have been made holy through the sacrifice of the body of Jesus Christ once for all.'

1 Peter 3:18
'For Christ also suffered once for sins, the righteous for the unrighteous to bring you to God. He was put to death in the body but made alive in the Spirit.'

1 Thessalonians 5:10
'He died for us so that, whether we are awake or asleep, we may live together with Him.'

2 Corinthians 5:15

'And He died for all, that those who live should no longer live for themselves but for Him who died for them and was raised again.'

Lord,

Thank You for sending Your perfect and blameless Son, Jesus to die on the cross for all my sins. I am so grateful that through the shedding of His blood, I can spend eternity with You. Thank You for helping me to understand that no amount of good works can make up for wrongs against You, but by believing in the price Jesus paid on the cross for my sins. Help me to have faith and place my trust in You. Forgive me for times when I am disobedient or act in ways which do not glorify You.

www.ingramcontent.com/pod-product-compliance
Lightning Source LLC
Chambersburg PA
CBHW071547080526
44588CB00011B/1825